WHAT YOUR NOSE KNOWS!

by Jane Belk Moncure
illustrated by Lois Axeman
created by The Child's World

CHILDRENS PRESS, CHICAGO

Cover and Title Page
Designed by Dolores Hollister

Library of Congress Cataloging in Publication Data

Moncure, Jane Belk.
What your nose knows!

(The Five senses)
Summary: Describes the many things your nose can identify throughout the year by their smells.
1. Smell — Juvenile literature. 2. Nose — Juvenile literature. [1. Smell. 2. Nose]
I. Axeman, Lois, ill. II. Title. III. Series:
Moncure, Jane Belk. Five senses.
QP458.M66 1982 152.1'66 82-9464
ISBN 0-516-03255-0 AACR2

WHAT YOUR NOSE KNOWS!

Your nose knows many things.
Even before you open the kitchen door,
your nose can tell you that Mom is baking a spice cake.

Spicy smells are all around you.

Even though your brother might not want you to know, your nose can tell you that he bought a warm brownie on his way home from school.

Your nose also can tell you
that your dog needs a bath and. . .

that some place close by, the ragweed grows, making you wheeze and sneeze.

And if a skunk should get frightened
in your back yard,
your nose certainly will know!

You cannot see smells.
But sometimes, just by sniffing,
your nose can tell the season of the year.
The flowery smells of . . .

apple blossoms,

lilacs, and

daffodils

tell you it is springtime.

And so does the rich-dirt smell
of your vegetable garden,

when you dig in it to plant some seeds.

Your nose knows
summer smells, too—
the woodsy smell of pines

when you're on a mountain hike. . .

the smells of the swimming pool. . .

and the mustard-and-onion smells
from the hot dog stand at the ball park.

Summer has special holiday smells as well.
By the burnt smell of fireworks exploding,
your nose knows it's the Fourth of July.

Jump into a pile of dry leaves.

The dusty-musty smell tells you it is fall.

Fall has special holiday smells as well.

The burnt-pumpkin smell of a
lighted jack-o-lantern
tells your nose it is Halloween.

Smell the turkey, cranberries,
and pumpkin pie!
Your nose knows
it is Thanksgiving Day!

Play in the snow on a frosty day.
The wet snow may tell your fingers and toes
that it is cold, cold winter.

But when you go inside,
it's the smell from the wood-burning fire
that tells your nose.

Winter has special holiday smells as well.
When your nose smells

bayberry candles,

a wreath of wintergreens,

a tree with popcorn chains and peppermint canes—
what do you know?
Yes! It's Christmas time!

Your nose knows when you are in the city.
You can smell

factories,

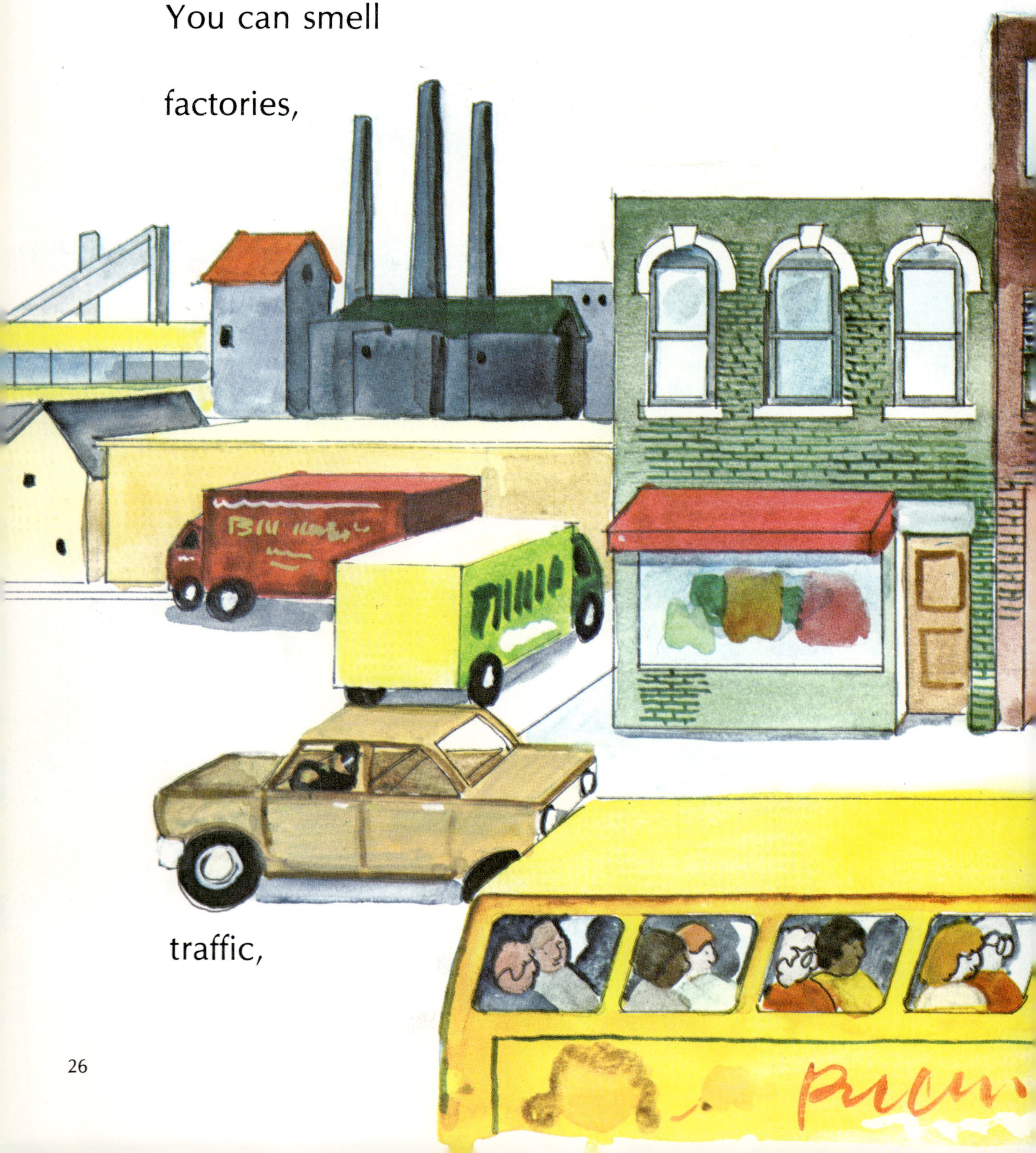

traffic,

and the spicy spaghetti sauce simmering
down at Mama Gina's restaurant.

Your nose knows when you
are in the country.
You can smell. . .

horses in the
pasture,

cows in the barn,

and hay
in the fields.

About the only time your
nose does not know a smell. . .
is when you are in bed
with a cold in your head!